WILD AND FREE

THE STORY
BLACK-FOOTED

by Jo-Ellen Bosson

Soundprints
PAPERBACKS

A Division of Trudy Management Corporation
Norwalk, Connecticut

For Stephanie, Jennifer, and Pam

Book Design: Johanna P. Shields

First Paperback Edition
10 9 8 7 6 5 4 3 2 1

Printed in Singapore

Library of Congress Cataloging-in-Publication Data

Bosson, Jo-Ellen, date.

Wild and free: the story of a black-footed ferret / by Jo-Ellen Bosson.
        p.   cm.
Summary: A black-footed ferret, bred in captivity and released in the wild,
tries to evade her natural enemies while raising her young in abandoned
prairie dog burrows.
     ISBN 0-924483-68-7   ISBN 156899-197-5 (pbk.)
1. Black-footed ferret — Juvenile fiction. [1. Black-footed ferret — Fiction.
2. Ferret — Fiction. 3. Rare animals — Fiction. 4. Prairie animals — Fiction.]
I. Title.
     PZ10.3.B656Wi 1992
     [E]—dc20   92-22797
                                                  AC

Prologue

*O*nce, millions of prairie dogs lived on the Great Plains, covering it with their "towns." Black-footed ferrets were there, too, preying on the prairie dogs and living in their burrows. When western settlers turned the prairie into farms and ranches, however, the habitat changed. So reduced were the numbers of prairie dogs and their towns that black-footed ferrets, dependent on them for food and shelter, began to disappear.

In the hope of saving an endangered species from extinction, wildlife experts captured the last few black-footed ferrets that they could find and bred them in captivity. When there were enough, some were released into the wild. This is a story about one of these animals.

The future of black-footed ferrets is still uncertain.

All is still. The prairie is sleeping beneath a
winter moon. Suddenly a small, agile form
bounds across the snow to a patch of shadow
and is hidden. It is a black-footed ferret,
hungry and hunting.

5

She dashes across open ground and disappears
down a prairie dog hole. Her keen sense of
smell tells her it is deserted. She quickly pops
out and pauses to check for danger. Then
she darts off again to hunt through the night.

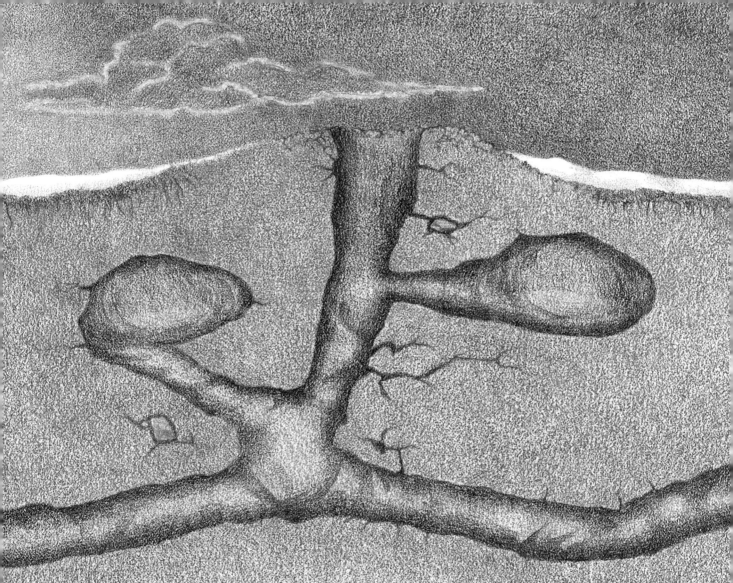

As the sun rises, she returns to her den in an old prairie dog burrow. The burrow's deep, warm tunnels and its safety exit will make it a good home for the kits that will soon be born.

Weeks pass, and spring has coaxed the prairie dogs out of hibernation. They eat the tender new grasses and wildflowers, then bask in the sun. Nearby, sage grouse dance in courtship. Their drumming sounds rise above the buzz of insects and prairie dog chatter. The prairie has come to life.

There is life below the sunny prairie, too. Four tiny ferret kits squirm in their warm burrow. Blind and helpless, they will stay in their nest for several weeks, nursing and sleeping. Their mother will leave them only when she needs to eat.

13

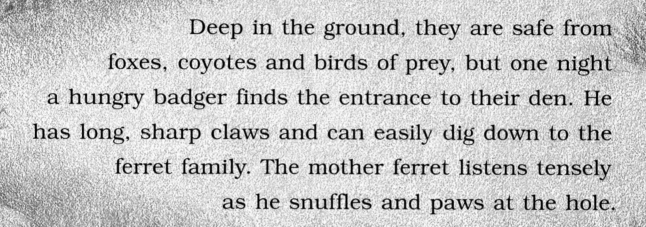

Deep in the ground, they are safe from
foxes, coyotes and birds of prey, but one night
a hungry badger finds the entrance to their den. He
has long, sharp claws and can easily dig down to the
ferret family. The mother ferret listens tensely
as he snuffles and paws at the hole.

Suddenly, an unlucky bull snake slithers
into the badger's sight. Here is a meal
without the bother of digging!
He pounces on the snake.

No longer hungry, the
badger ambles off,
leaving the ferrets
undisturbed.

Now the mother ferret does not feel
safe in this den. An enemy has
found it! She finds a clean,
empty prairie dog burrow
and gently carries her kits
there, one by one. She
will change dens many
times as her kits grow.

A month passes, and the kits are ready to eat meat.
Now the mother ferret must hunt constantly. It is hard
work. The prairie dogs she hunts often outweigh her
and have sharp teeth and claws. She must catch them
in their tunnels, where there is little room for them
to turn and fight.

Finally the kits are old enough to leave their den, but they are timid and afraid. Their mother calls to them with soft, begging grunts, and soon three little faces peer out of the hole. Cautiously, they creep out onto the prairie.

But the last kit is too fearful, and the world is too big and strange. The mother ferret gently tugs him to coax him out. Soon all four are following mother, bounding across the prairie single file, heading for a new den.

Almost grown, the kits play near the den in the morning sun.
They race madly back and forth, pouncing on one another
and wrestling in furry heaps. This is a time, too, to practice
hunting. They attack weeds, insects, and each other's tails.

Caught up in play, they do not see the golden eagle that is looking for breakfast. Mother ferret is alert. She chatters a sharp warning as the eagle swoops toward her kits. Just in time, they all dive for the safety of the burrow.

As summer ends, the mother ferret places her kits in four separate dens. This is the beginning of their solitary, adult lives. One night when she brings food, she finds their burrows empty. Her work is over; the kits are grown and have gone to live free and wild on the open prairie.

About the Black-footed Ferret

Now one of the most endangered mammals in North America, black-footed ferrets once lived successfully among the vast colonies of prairie dogs on the Great Plains. They fed on small reptiles, birds, and rodents — principally the prairie dogs themselves. As farms, ranches, and other developments began to displace many of the prairie dog "towns," the black-footed ferret lost both its home and principal food source. Today, there are only a few tiny populations left — and these were established with animals taken into and bred in captivity.

Glossary

badger: member of the Mustelidae family, and a relative of the skunk and weasel. Badgers are powerful diggers who are easily recognized by the white stripe that runs from their shoulders to the end of their upturned, pointed noses.

bull snake: a large, harmless snake that feeds chiefly on rodents.

burrow: a hole in the ground, dug by an animal for shelter.

den: space, such as a cave, niche, hollow log, or dugout, used by an animal for shelter.

kits: the young of several kinds of mammals, including ferrets.

prairie: relatively flat grassland with few trees.

prairie dog: a highly vocal and sociable relative of the squirrel that lives in colonies (sometimes called "towns") on the western plains and is best known for its distinctive, dog-like bark. While prairie dogs will occasionally eat insects and very small animals, they are primarily vegetarian.

ranch: a farm with a particular specialty, such as raising horses, beef cattle, or sheep.

sage grouse: a large, plump bird of the western plains with mottled gray and buff plumage and a black belly.

species: kind; sort; a category of biological classification.

Points of Interest in this Book

pp. 12-13 Born almost hairless, black-footed ferrets are covered by silvery white fuzz within a few days. Adult markings develop gradually during their first four to six weeks.

pp. 14, 25 White evening primrose.

pp. 22-23 By the time they are ready to venture from the den for the first time, black-footed ferrets are already one-half to two-thirds the size of their mother.

p. 27 Purple prairie clover.